The Sun

by Ruth Renolo

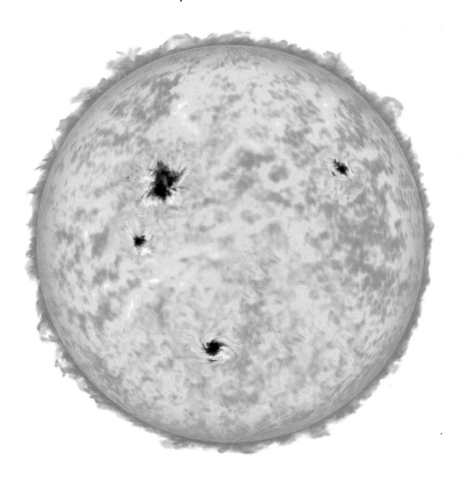

PEARSON
Scott
Foresman

DK

What You Already Know

The Sun gives Earth light and heat. Living things need these to live and grow. The Sun is a star. Stars are big balls of hot gas.

The Sun is bigger than Earth. Earth moves around the Sun. It turns around and around. This is rotation. Earth makes one rotation a day. Rotation causes day and night. Day is when one side of Earth faces the Sun.

Earth is a planet. It moves around the Sun. Other planets do too. Planets do not give off light like stars do. A telescope helps us to see far-away planets.

The Moon moves around Earth.
We see the Moon mostly at night.
The Moon does not have air,
plants, or animals. We see the
part of the Moon lit by the
Sun. The Moon looks a
little different each night.
It looks the same again
each twenty-nine days
or so.

Things in space look
small because they are far
away. The Sun can look
small to us, but it is not.
Read on to find out more
about the Sun and why it
is so important to Earth.

The Sun

The Sun is a big, hot ball of gas. It is the closest star to Earth. Earth and the Sun are in the same solar system. The Sun is in the center. Everything in the solar system moves around the Sun.

The Sun is very important to our planet.

Earth is just the right distance from the Sun. The Sun is not too far away. Its light feels warm. But the light is not too hot. The Sun keeps Earth from being cold and dark all the time. Nothing could live here without the light that comes through space from the Sun.

The Sun Gives Light

The light of the Sun is very strong. It makes lots of heat. Too much sunlight can be dangerous. We should protect our skin and eyes from the Sun.

We can see the Sun's strong light in the daytime. But did you know we even see light from the Sun at night? The Moon lights up at night because light from the Sun bounces off it.

Clothes, hats, and sunglasses protect people from the Sun.

Earth would be dark without the Sun.

Day and Night

Earth is always moving. Earth turns and turns as it goes around the Sun. The Sun lights one side of Earth at a time. The side turned to the Sun is lit. The side turned away is dark.

It is day on the lit side. It is night on the dark side. Then Earth turns. Night becomes day and day becomes night. The Sun is not gone at night. It is shining on the other side of Earth. We just cannot see it!

One side of Earth has day when the other side has night.

The Sun Gives Heat

The light from the Sun causes heat when it shines on something. This is how the Sun's light heats Earth.

Some places on Earth are heated by the Sun's light more than other places.

Some people go to the beach when it is hot outside.

The curve of Earth makes the Sun's rays hit in different ways in different places. The rays hit straight down on the middle of Earth. These places can be very hot. The rays do not hit straight down on the top and bottom of Earth. These places can be very cold.

The Sun Gives Energy

Plants use the Sun's light. They use it to live, grow, and make their own food. Other living things cannot make their own food. These other living things may eat plants to get energy. Living things also can get energy when they eat animals that have eaten plants. Plants give energy from the Sun to other living things.

This sunflower plant gets energy from the Sun.

The Sun in the Center

    Our planet would be a very different place without the light of this important star. Every living thing on Earth needs the Sun. The Sun is the center of our solar system.

There are times we cannot see the Sun in the sky. But we know that it is always there. We also know that things on Earth will live and grow because the Sun is there.

Glossary

bounce   spring back after hitting something

center   the middle

curve   a line with no straight part

solar system the Sun and all the planets, moons, and other things that revolve around it

space   all the area around Earth